S

Nam

11000

------Amiesk Book Publications------

RAM RAM RAM RAM RAM RAM RAM RAM RAM RAM RAM RAM RAM RAM RAM RAM RAM RAM RAM RAM RAM RAM RAM RAM RAM RAM RAM RAM

RAM RAM RAM RAM RAM RAM RAM RAM RAM RAM RAM RAM RAM RAM RAM RAM RAM RAM RAM RAM RAM RAM RAM RAM

------Amiesk Book Publications------

We would love to have feedback from you. Get in touch with us at :

E·mail id : amieskbook@gmail·com
Blog : amieskbooks·blogspot·in
Facebook : @amieskbooks

The painting on the cover page is Original work of Amrita Gupta.

Designer: Amrita Gupta

RAM RAM RAM RAM RAM RAM RAM RAM

RAM RAM RAM RAM RAM RAM RAM RAM

RAM RAM RAM RAM RAM RAM RAM RAM

RAM RAM RAM RAM RAM RAM RAM RAM

RAM RAM RAM RAM RAM RAM RAM RAM

RAM RAM RAM RAM RAM RAM RAM RAM

RAM RAM RAM RAM RAM RAM RAM RAM

RAM RAM RAM RAM RAM RAM RAM RAM

RAM RAM RAM RAM RAM RAM RAM RAM

RAM RAM RAM RAM RAM RAM RAM RAM

RAM RAM RAM RAM RAM RAM RAM RAM

RAM RAM RAM RAM RAM RAM RAM RAM

RAM RAM RAM RAM RAM RAM RAM RAM

RAM RAM RAM RAM RAM RAM RAM RAM

RAM RAM RAM RAM RAM RAM RAM RAM

RAM RAM RAM RAM RAM RAM RAM RAM

RAM RAM RAM RAM RAM RAM RAM RAM

RAM RAM RAM RAM RAM RAM RAM RAM

RAM RAM RAM RAM RAM RAM RAM RAM

RAM RAM RAM RAM RAM RAM RAM RAM

RAM RAM RAM RAM RAM RAM RAM RAM

RAM RAM RAM RAM RAM RAM RAM RAM

RAM RAM RAM RAM RAM RAM RAM RAM

RAM RAM RAM RAM RAM RAM RAM RAM

RAM RAM RAM RAM RAM RAM RAM RAM

RAM RAM RAM RAM RAM RAM RAM RAM

RAM RAM RAM RAM RAM RAM RAM RAM

RAM RAM RAM RAM RAM RAM RAM RAM

RAM RAM RAM RAM RAM RAM RAM RAM

RAM RAM RAM RAM RAM RAM RAM RAM

RAM RAM RAM RAM RAM RAM RAM RAM

RAM RAM RAM RAM RAM RAM RAM RAM

RAM RAM RAM RAM RAM RAM RAM RAM

RAM RAM RAM RAM RAM RAM RAM RAM

RAM RAM RAM RAM RAM RAM RAM RAM

RAM RAM RAM RAM RAM RAM RAM RAM

RAM RAM RAM RAM RAM RAM RAM RAM

RAM RAM RAM RAM RAM RAM RAM RAM

RAM RAM RAM RAM RAM RAM RAM RAM

RAM RAM RAM RAM RAM RAM RAM RAM

RAM RAM RAM RAM RAM RAM RAM RAM

RAM RAM RAM RAM RAM RAM RAM RAM

RAM RAM RAM RAM RAM RAM RAM RAM

RAM RAM RAM RAM RAM RAM RAM RAM

RAM RAM RAM RAM RAM RAM RAM RAM

RAM RAM RAM RAM RAM RAM RAM RAM

RAM RAM RAM RAM RAM RAM RAM RAM

RAM RAM RAM RAM RAM RAM RAM RAM

RAM RAM RAM RAM RAM RAM RAM RAM

RAM RAM RAM RAM RAM RAM RAM RAM

RAM RAM RAM RAM RAM RAM RAM RAM

RAM RAM RAM RAM RAM RAM RAM RAM

RAM RAM RAM RAM RAM RAM RAM RAM

RAM RAM RAM RAM RAM RAM RAM RAM

RAM RAM RAM RAM RAM RAM RAM RAM

RAM RAM RAM RAM RAM RAM RAM RAM

RAM RAM RAM RAM RAM RAM RAM RAM

RAM RAM RAM RAM RAM RAM RAM RAM

RAM RAM RAM RAM RAM RAM RAM RAM

RAM RAM RAM RAM RAM RAM RAM RAM

RAM RAM RAM RAM RAM RAM RAM RAM

RAM RAM RAM RAM RAM RAM RAM RAM

RAM RAM RAM RAM RAM RAM RAM RAM

RAM RAM RAM RAM RAM RAM RAM RAM

RAM RAM RAM RAM RAM RAM RAM RAM

RAM RAM RAM RAM RAM RAM RAM RAM

RAM RAM RAM RAM RAM RAM RAM RAM

RAM RAM RAM RAM RAM RAM RAM RAM

RAM RAM RAM RAM RAM RAM RAM RAM

RAM RAM RAM RAM RAM RAM RAM RAM

RAM RAM RAM RAM RAM RAM RAM RAM

RAM RAM RAM RAM RAM RAM RAM RAM

RAM RAM RAM RAM RAM RAM RAM RAM

RAM RAM RAM RAM RAM RAM RAM RAM

RAM RAM RAM RAM RAM RAM RAM RAM

RAM RAM RAM RAM RAM RAM RAM RAM

RAM RAM RAM RAM RAM RAM RAM RAM

RAM RAM RAM RAM RAM RAM RAM RAM

RAM RAM RAM RAM RAM RAM RAM RAM

RAM RAM RAM RAM RAM RAM RAM RAM

RAM RAM RAM RAM RAM RAM RAM RAM

RAM RAM RAM RAM RAM RAM RAM RAM

RAM RAM RAM RAM RAM RAM RAM RAM

RAM RAM RAM RAM RAM RAM RAM RAM

RAM RAM RAM RAM RAM RAM RAM RAM

RAM RAM RAM RAM RAM RAM RAM RAM

RAM RAM RAM RAM RAM RAM RAM RAM

RAM RAM RAM RAM RAM RAM RAM RAM

RAM RAM RAM RAM RAM RAM RAM RAM

RAM RAM RAM RAM RAM RAM RAM RAM

RAM RAM RAM RAM RAM RAM RAM RAM

RAM RAM RAM RAM RAM RAM RAM RAM

RAM RAM RAM RAM RAM RAM RAM RAM

RAM RAM RAM RAM RAM RAM RAM RAM

RAM RAM RAM RAM RAM RAM RAM RAM

RAM RAM RAM RAM RAM RAM RAM RAM

RAM RAM RAM RAM RAM RAM RAM RAM

RAM RAM RAM RAM RAM RAM RAM RAM

RAM RAM RAM RAM RAM RAM RAM RAM

RAM RAM RAM RAM RAM RAM RAM RAM

RAM RAM RAM RAM RAM RAM RAM RAM

RAM RAM RAM RAM RAM RAM RAM RAM

RAM RAM RAM RAM RAM RAM RAM RAM

RAM RAM RAM RAM RAM RAM RAM RAM

RAM RAM RAM RAM RAM RAM RAM RAM

RAM RAM RAM RAM RAM RAM RAM RAM

RAM RAM RAM RAM RAM RAM RAM RAM

RAM RAM RAM RAM RAM RAM RAM RAM

RAM RAM RAM RAM RAM RAM RAM RAM

RAM RAM RAM RAM RAM RAM RAM RAM

RAM RAM RAM RAM RAM RAM RAM RAM

RAM RAM RAM RAM RAM RAM RAM RAM

RAM RAM RAM RAM RAM RAM RAM RAM

RAM RAM RAM RAM RAM RAM RAM RAM

RAM RAM RAM RAM RAM RAM RAM RAM

RAM RAM RAM RAM RAM RAM RAM RAM

RAM RAM RAM RAM RAM RAM RAM RAM

RAM RAM RAM RAM RAM RAM RAM RAM

RAM RAM RAM RAM RAM RAM RAM RAM

RAM RAM RAM RAM RAM RAM RAM RAM

RAM RAM RAM RAM RAM RAM RAM RAM

RAM RAM RAM RAM RAM RAM RAM RAM

RAM RAM RAM RAM RAM RAM RAM RAM

RAM RAM RAM RAM RAM RAM RAM RAM

RAM RAM RAM RAM RAM RAM RAM RAM

RAM RAM RAM RAM RAM RAM RAM RAM

RAM RAM RAM RAM RAM RAM RAM RAM

RAM RAM RAM RAM RAM RAM RAM RAM

RAM RAM RAM RAM RAM RAM RAM RAM

RAM RAM RAM RAM RAM RAM RAM RAM

RAM RAM RAM RAM RAM RAM RAM RAM

RAM RAM RAM RAM RAM RAM RAM RAM

RAM RAM RAM RAM RAM RAM RAM RAM

RAM RAM RAM RAM RAM RAM RAM RAM

RAM RAM RAM RAM RAM RAM RAM RAM

RAM RAM RAM RAM RAM RAM RAM RAM

RAM RAM RAM RAM RAM RAM RAM RAM

RAM RAM RAM RAM RAM RAM RAM RAM

RAM RAM RAM RAM RAM RAM RAM RAM

RAM RAM RAM RAM RAM RAM RAM RAM

RAM RAM RAM RAM RAM RAM RAM RAM

RAM RAM RAM RAM RAM RAM RAM RAM

RAM RAM RAM RAM RAM RAM RAM RAM

RAM RAM RAM RAM RAM RAM RAM RAM

RAM RAM RAM RAM RAM RAM RAM RAM

RAM RAM RAM RAM RAM RAM RAM RAM

RAM RAM RAM RAM RAM RAM RAM RAM

RAM RAM RAM RAM RAM RAM RAM RAM

RAM RAM RAM RAM RAM RAM RAM RAM

RAM RAM RAM RAM RAM RAM RAM RAM

RAM RAM RAM RAM RAM RAM RAM RAM

RAM RAM RAM RAM RAM RAM RAM RAM

RAM RAM RAM RAM RAM RAM RAM RAM

RAM RAM RAM RAM RAM RAM RAM RAM

RAM RAM RAM RAM RAM RAM RAM RAM

RAM RAM RAM RAM RAM RAM RAM RAM

RAM RAM RAM RAM RAM RAM RAM RAM

RAM RAM RAM RAM RAM RAM RAM RAM

RAM RAM RAM RAM RAM RAM RAM RAM

RAM RAM RAM RAM RAM RAM RAM RAM

RAM RAM RAM RAM RAM RAM RAM RAM

RAM RAM RAM RAM RAM RAM RAM RAM

RAM RAM RAM RAM RAM RAM RAM RAM

RAM RAM RAM RAM RAM RAM RAM RAM

RAM RAM RAM RAM RAM RAM RAM RAM

RAM RAM RAM RAM RAM RAM RAM RAM

RAM RAM RAM RAM RAM RAM RAM RAM

RAM RAM RAM RAM RAM RAM RAM RAM

RAM RAM RAM RAM RAM RAM RAM RAM

RAM RAM RAM RAM RAM RAM RAM RAM

RAM RAM RAM RAM RAM RAM RAM RAM

RAM RAM RAM RAM RAM RAM RAM RAM

RAM RAM RAM RAM RAM RAM RAM RAM

RAM RAM RAM RAM RAM RAM RAM RAM

RAM RAM RAM RAM RAM RAM RAM RAM

RAM RAM RAM RAM RAM RAM RAM RAM

RAM RAM RAM RAM RAM RAM RAM RAM

RAM RAM RAM RAM RAM RAM RAM RAM

RAM RAM RAM RAM RAM RAM RAM RAM

RAM RAM RAM RAM RAM RAM RAM RAM

RAM RAM RAM RAM RAM RAM RAM RAM

RAM RAM RAM RAM RAM RAM RAM RAM

RAM RAM RAM RAM RAM RAM RAM RAM

RAM RAM RAM RAM RAM RAM RAM RAM

RAM RAM RAM RAM RAM RAM RAM RAM

RAM RAM RAM RAM RAM RAM RAM RAM

RAM RAM RAM RAM RAM RAM RAM RAM

RAM RAM RAM RAM RAM RAM RAM RAM

RAM RAM RAM RAM RAM RAM RAM RAM

RAM RAM RAM RAM RAM RAM RAM RAM

RAM RAM RAM RAM RAM RAM RAM RAM

RAM RAM RAM RAM RAM RAM RAM RAM

RAM RAM RAM RAM RAM RAM RAM RAM

RAM RAM RAM RAM RAM RAM RAM RAM

RAM RAM RAM RAM RAM RAM RAM RAM

RAM RAM RAM RAM RAM RAM RAM RAM

RAM RAM RAM RAM RAM RAM RAM RAM

RAM RAM RAM RAM RAM RAM RAM RAM

RAM RAM RAM RAM RAM RAM RAM RAM

RAM RAM RAM RAM RAM RAM RAM RAM

RAM RAM RAM RAM RAM RAM RAM RAM

RAM RAM RAM RAM RAM RAM RAM RAM

SHRI RAM

Name Writing Book

11000

------Amiesk Book Publications------

RAM RAM RAM RAM RAM RAM RAM RAM RAM RAM RAM RAM RAM RAM RAM RAM RAM RAM RAM RAM RAM RAM RAM RAM RAM RAM RAM RAM

RAM RAM RAM RAM RAM RAM RAM RAM RAM RAM RAM RAM RAM RAM RAM RAM RAM RAM RAM RAM RAM RAM RAM RAM RAM RAM RAM RAM

Made in the USA
Middletown, DE
03 May 2021

38912733R00060